FACE PAINTING 101

A True Step by Step Beginners Guide to Becoming a Professional Face Painter

written by Nancy J. Duso

FACE PAINTING 101

A True Step by Step Beginners Guide to Becoming a Professional Face Painter

ISBN: 978-1-105-83449-3

Dedication and Thanks

I love the idea of passing it on to other beginning face painters because so many Professional face painters helped me learn and grow as a painter. Many thanks to Heather from Silly Farm for her encouragement and training that she so freely gives to others.

Also I want to thank my wonderful husband, Rich for giving me a face and body to always practice on, and serving as a great manager of our tent at all events that we did. You always encouraged me to be the best.

Special thanks to Alyssa for allowing me to paint her pretty face.

I also want to thank my friend Jean Marie, without whom I never would have written this book, for all your training and encouragement and the best of friendships.

A friend is one of the nicest things you can have,
and one of the best things you can be !

Happy Painting
Live, Laugh, Love,

Nancy

Table of Contents

Intro

Face Painting is quite a bit different than painting on a canvas or a wall. You now will have a moving breathing wiggle worm in your chair.
You will need proper brushes and paints made to use on skin. Face and Boy Art Make-up. No acrylics or enamels here.

This little book has been created for decorative painters that are moving from painting on canvas, glass, etc...guiding you to painting on a person, as well as how to set up your table and chair, all the way to what to charge for an event. I also included 6 quick easy designs and some practice tips. At the very end you will learn how to clean up your brushes and paints and places to purchase your products.

So let's get started!

Setting up your area to paint

Arrangement of your chair, table and supplies is kind of personal, everybody has a different idea of what works for them. My choices are usually guided by how comfortable I can make it for my body. Trust me when I say that I have tried the two folding chairs sitting across from each other, and by the end of the day I am in serious back pain.

So then, my choice is a rectangle table that easily folds in half, covered by a cute easy to clean tablecloth. A director chair, or a tall bar stool with a back works well. I usually attach a small trash bag to my chair.

Arrangement for a right hander, (switch for a lefty) I have found the most comfortable way to paint is to stand on a cushioned mat, table on my left at a diagonal, chair on my right facing the party-goers so the moms, dads, and friends can watch their child or friend as you paint, and stay out of your way.

*Standing with a straight back on a gel mat saves your back and legs.

What goes on your Table
Your Painting Kit :

Glitter (light multicolor is best to start)
Powders (details coming up)
Brush holder full of brushes
several smoothie blenders
pack of business cards
hand mirror
Stencils (dolphin & fairy are good to have)
baggie of hair clippies (they keep -no sharing)
hand sanitizer
Q-tips (for lipstick)

Other items you will need to have:

(2) - half full cups of water –
one for rinsing brushes, one for dipping
into before you add paint
Q-tips (for lipstick)
Mini spray bottle of water
Duck tape - I love the multicolored ones
Net bag full of sponges cut in half
large gallon baggie for used sponges
baby wipes (un-scented)
Picture choices –for kids to choose from
brush holder for multiple brushes
bean filled small tub (put smoothie blenders in)
Larger mirror for kids to look in after
        they get out of your chair –

Paint Palette

When it comes to which brand of paint to use,
there are so many choices. I have tried out quite a few over the
past 11 yrs. Since I live in a hot humid climate I mostly use
Paradise paint, rainbow cakes and powders.

My top favorites are the mulit-colored rainbow cakes from
Silly Farm ™ and Paradise paint is from Mehron ™.
Remember this paint is cosmetic make-up, not craft paint.

When you start out you will need at least the basic colors,
these are the most used colors in my kit.

> White, red, pink, yellow, purple, green
> light, green dark, blue light, black,
> add more colors as you grow.....

The powders are dry, and put onto face using a smoothie blender.
I find the Star bend from Mehron™ and Snazaroo™ sparkle
powders is the fastest and easiest to use, and the most used
colors are:

> White, red, orange, yellow, pink, green,
> black, add more as you grow...

Don't forget to have a couple of cakes that have multi-colors in
them Rainbow cakes or the little Arty cakes

Star blend™ Powders and sparkle powders are similar to eye
shadows - come in many colors choices **No water needed**

Brushes

Brushes like the paint come in many different flavors – depending upon what you want – Big and bold tiger lines, or pretty dainty lines for eye candy. Make sure you keep your Face Painting brushes separate from any others.

Synthetic brushes are ideal for face painters because they withstand repeated use in water, daily cleaning, and load and distribute face and body make up evenly.

I recommend starting out with at least the following to get you started:

1 – ¾ Flat
1 - #12 flat
1 - # 6 round
2 - # 4 round
1 - # 2 round
1 – liner
4 - Smoothie Blenders

To get the most of your brushes, store in a place that will not bend the tips or flatten the bristles. It is recommended that you do not leave your brushes soaking in water because you will bend the tips and cause separation of the bristle hairs

Loading a brush and sponge correctly.

Loading a brush –
Dip the brush in the water, then stroke the brush back and forth over the paint

If your wanting to make tiger lines or outline your design, you normally want to start with a thin line so your brush should be in a point

If your wanting a tear drop, flatten your brush as you load the paint.

Loading a sponge –

To load a sponge you can <u>either</u> wet the sponge and wring it out VERY well, then rub across your paint , or you can wet the paint and then rub the sponge across the paint. Try it both ways see which you like best. I have done both and it works either way. Most important is not to have the sponge too wet or the paint will be dripping off their face.

Using Powders

Yes, as you can imagine there are a lot of different types of powders that can be used. Star Blend by Mehron™ is one I use all the time. Using one of your smoothie blenders, rub the top of the powder, which is a matte finish hard powder. Then you smooth it on the area of the face. Great for a quick tiger face, or monster mask, or spidy.

Now, the pretty sparkle powder is loose and is made by Snazaroo™ and you use a smoothie blender to rub it on the face, used like an eye shadow, it is usually a more shimmer finish.

While most all powders are used dry, I have seen some use the Star Blend™ wet. Though I don't think you can go back to dry afterwards.

Just a short word on Glitter you need to use a polyester cosmetic glitter excellent for adding that extra touch of sparkle to your face and it comes in many colors.

Pics of My Kit

Here are a couple shots of what my kit looks like and what I need on my table. Just so you can see what I'm talking about.

All items (except for the container with the beans) fit in my little box.

Closed Kit, Net bag full of sponges, water spray, small container of pinto beans for smoothie blenders

And something to keep it all in, on wheels works well.

Practice, Practice and more Practice.....

Never enough practice, we can always improve upon the last time. Remember you are not in a competition with me or anyone else, your goal is to improve upon the last one <u>you</u> did.

Practice, practice, practice. The first time you paint the tiger face, for example, it will take you 10 to 15 min. After painting it 10 times you will have it down to 5 or 6 min. After painting it 100 times you will easily have it down to 3 to 5 min. An experienced painter can paint this face in 3-5 min.

You can practice on wax paper taped down with some masking tape, this would be good to practice tiger lines, tear drops and swirls. Example of this on the next couple of pages.

Might want to also pick up a doll head to practice your face designs on. Sometimes you can find them at a Beauty school.

Time to Pick up your Brush and Start Practicing....

Copy what you see here and on the next couple of pages onto a piece of wax paper or a white board will work too, remember to hold your brush straight up and down like a ballet slipper on point, as you move the brush start laying the <u>bristles</u> of the brush down for the thick part then bring back up to the tippy toe again.

Just keep **SLOWLY** moving your brush as you make the <u>bristles</u> put down paint thin and thick.

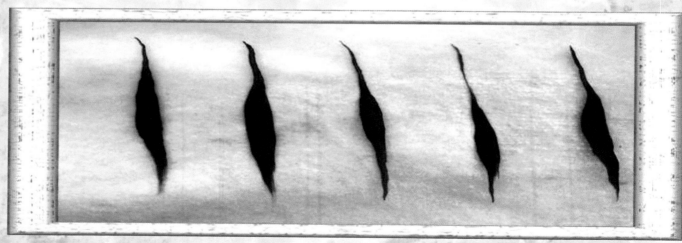

Tiger Lines Practice

Again copy what I did here onto your wax paper or whatever you decide to paint on. If you practice every day for a couple of weeks — like 10 min a day — you will make your face painting look fantastic.

Swirls N Curls

I put down a piece of wax paper, lined in with masking tape and started practicing thick and thin swirls

Tear Drop Practice

You can never practice too much, while your watching TV, practice on your leg. All you need is a brush, cup of water, white paint, and a baby wipe.

Remember you are going to be doing this on the face and you need a focal point.

Four focal points on a face are right between the eyes, the corner of each eye, and the chin.

All of the points that your tear drops point towards. Practice putting a dot on the paper – then starting with a flattened brush moving towards the dot bringing your brush to a point. Takes practice but you can do it.

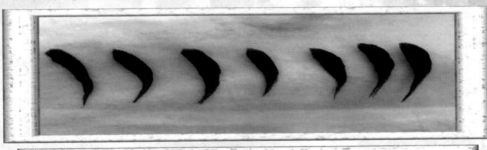

Swirls and Tear Drops

Now put them together the way you might use on a face or arm design.

Practicing on a person

When you get your first child in your chair, I talk to them, find out what they like, colors they want – give the child 2 choices – pick something you want to paint; for ex: princess or butterfly, remember <u>YOU'RE in charge</u>, if they choose something you don't know how to do, simply say "today we are doing princesses and butterflies".

I ask them to close their eyes, softly place my hand on their head, keeping their chin up and facing me, then start placing your base down with a sponge or brush, outline your design, don't forget the glitter, show them their face and help them down.

Remember their head turned up towards you is much easier on your back, they will only be in the chair for a few min, you'll be there lots longer. A booster seat helps too.

Fast Easy Design #1
Bat boy

Here I used a round #6 placing a M in the middle of the forehead curving the outline of the wings, coming back under the eyes to a point on the nose. Place 2 yellow dots for eyes the boys love it.

Fast Easy Design #2
Butterfly

 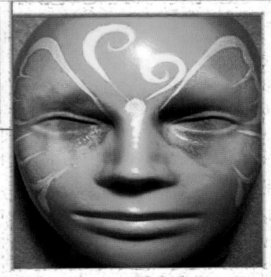

Load your sponge with your favorite rainbow cake, place on face like a triangle for top 2 wings, then to smaller triangles for the bottom wings. Outline everything in white, some dots in the center, and 2 swirls coming from the center. Don't forget to add glitter.

Careful - too much water and the paint will run down the face.

Powder Base #3
Butterfly Face

Here is a butterfly example using a powder base then outline is done with paint. I used some of the curls n swirls you practiced.

Fast Easy Design #4
Skull mask

Used a sponge to lay down the white, and a 6 round for all but the thin cracks and I used a liner for those.

Fast Easy Design #5
Little Princess

Used a rainbow cake loaded on a ¾ " brush , switched
to a 4 round for the dots, teardrops, and flower.
Don't forget glitter !

Fast and Easy
Rainbow Kitty # 6

Using the rounded side of the sponge I loaded the paint –
then loaded white on the top edge, keeping the white side
going down the middle of the face from eyebrow to the
corner of the mouth. Rolling the sponge with the color
towards the outside.

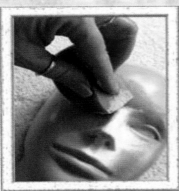 

As you paint the fur
down the side of
the face. remember
to curve as the face
is rounded.

Fast N Easy Tiger # 7

When your loading your sponge to lay down the base for your tiger, you'll notice it's the same as the kitty. Its different in that you will lay the color all the way around the face again you keep the white in the center. The tiger line practice that we did a couple of pages ago is what you will put in the center of the forehead. Then use thick and thin lines for the tiger strips. On this simple version, I didn't outline the muzzle, but I did give him teeth, boys love that.

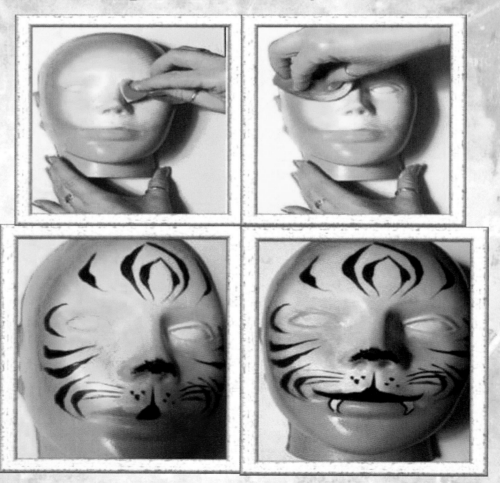

How to know what to Charge

Now that you have spent all this money buying the face paints, brushes and had some time to practice. Lets get to how much to charge. It's one of the most asked questions from new face painters. "How do I know what to charge?"

If you are adding face painting to your creative painting, or to your entertainment business then just go by your hourly rate. I usually give businesses a discount of some sort because then they may use you every year for their event.

Pay per face events are not my favorite because then I have to deal with collecting and giving money. However, when you do the basic rate is whatever the price of the beer is. I know that sounds silly, but the rule of thumb is if they are willing to pay $4 for a beer they will pay $4 for a child to get a painted face.

Call around to other entertainers in the area, see what their basic rate is. If your just starting out you don't want to over price yourself. Word of mouth is the best form of advertisement. Know someone that has kids, offer to paint faces at their birthday party for 10% off.

Parties and Events

Ok – It's time to book your first party and you need to know certain things before you get there in order to do a great job, and get a good recommendation from them.

Here are the basic questions I ask
<u>before I accept an event of any kind:</u>

Date: Are you available? Check your calendar
Time: Start & finish
Place: how far from home – gas charge?
How many guests: 5 min ea person at least
General Age of guests: will guide your face choices
Inside or Outside event: will you need a tent?
Theme: ex: zoo –have animal faces ready to choose from.

If the person says they are having about **60** kids and he only gives you **2** hours, you know that is not enough time for just one face painter.

Make sure you get a deposit for the event if its longer than a week away, this deposit assures that you will hold that date and time <u>for them</u>, and will not book any other event during that time. This is done to <u>protect their booking,</u> as well as protect you from last-minute cancellations that could incur losses from other jobs you may have had to turn away.
I usually send them an invoice via PayPal™

Your Time

Your time is important and I wanted to add some things you will run across continually.

Donating your time to face paint for our charitable event – This is really a hard one..
It's something I get asked a lot, and while I absolutely love using my skills for good causes, I must limit the amount of time I donate to charities. <u>However</u>, I am willing to work for a reduced rate -<u>OR</u> - I can charge a per face and donate a portion of the proceeds to their organization.

How far in advance should you book –
It's never too early to book! You should book your event <u>as soon as you know the time and date</u>. Weekends fill up fast.

Why hire a Professional Face Painter –
It's true that you will pay more for a skilled professional face painter, but in many ways YOU come out well ahead. I am able to paint much more quickly than a hobby or volunteer painter. I spend hours practicing my skills so that when hired I can provide fast, *high quality* designs. As a *professional*, I am also very experienced in handling large crowds of children. I use <u>top-quality FDA compliant cosmetic make-up and glitter</u>, which is extremely important for the safety of their children.

What to wear

I remember back when I started I got a pair of coveralls to use as my costume, I put cute colored pockets and fru-fru on it. Painted my face up like a butterfly or cat and went out to paint. While that was fine, it wasn't very comfortable for hours that I worked an event.

Now I simply wear a painted scrub shirt, pants, comfortable shoes and a cute fuzzy hair thing.

The kids and parents want to see clean, neat and a friendly smile on your face.

Clean Kit

This has got to be one of the most important parts of this little book. Having a clean kit not only looks more professional and attractive, it keeps the germs away.

When your done for the day take a baby wipe and wipe all your paints down. This way all of your paints are clean and smooth again.

The large baggie I keep my used sponges in, I also put all my brushes in to clean in hot soapy water when I get home.

I use a bar of "The Master's" ™ soap to clean all my sponges and brushes under hot water till they look clean and new again. After a bit they get stains that no longer come out – I toss them out. As you clean your brushes reform the bristles so when they dry they are ready to go.

Store your <u>completely</u> dried sponges in a net bag so they don't get bacteria, and store dried brushes in your brush holder in your kit.

The Right Stuff

SillyFarm.com is pretty much the easiest place to one-stop-shop. They have it all plus video's to show you the latest designs. Great customer service if you call, easy to order on-line.

Dollar Store has the little things like
Q-tips, hand mirror, net bag, hair clippies, baggies, little container for the beans, hand sanitizer, gum

Dewberry Crafts ™ has great tools to practice your lines, brushes, and face paints

Donnas' plastic sleeves work great for practicing your tear drops and lines, I find her Scroll recipe card is very similar to the tear drops for princesses

These are by no means the only place to shop, but they are the places I shop to purchase all my face paints, powders, brushes, etc....

About the Author

Nancy Duso, owner of Paint a Pretty Face, has been sharing her creativity and love for others as a local face painting artist and teacher since 2001. Her face-painting designs have delighted thousands of children across Central Florida at fairs, festivals, and other public events. She is also one of the founders of the face painting ministry at Calvary Chapel of Melbourne.

Recently mentored by Donna Dewberry, a well-known crafter and painting instructor, Nancy is also a "One Stroke Certified Instructor." Nancy met Donna at the Face Painting Convention in 2011, and fell in love with her style of painting.Now she is enjoying the easy relaxed One Stroke ™ painting style in her own backyard.

As a Face Painting Instructor and as an OSC1 instructor, Nancy loves to express her joy of painting while sharing her faith with others. Introducing her students to the wonderful world of painting, her students learn to blend, highlight and shade, all in one stroke and are amazed at what they can create in just a few hours.

Find Nancy on the website for her calendar of events

WWW.PAINTAPRETTYFACE.COM